D1568700

THE SHAKER VILLAGE

THE
SHAKER VILLAGE

RAYMOND BIAL

THE UNIVERSITY PRESS OF KENTUCKY

Scholarly publisher for the Commonwealth,
serving Bellarmine University, Berea College, Centre
College of Kentucky, Eastern Kentucky University,
The Filson Historical Society, Georgetown College,
Kentucky Historical Society, Kentucky State University,
Morehead State University, Murray State University,
Northern Kentucky University, Transylvania University,
University of Kentucky, University of Louisville,
and Western Kentucky University.
All rights reserved.

Editorial and Sales Offices: The University Press of Kentucky
663 South Limestone Street, Lexington, Kentucky 40508-4008
www.kentuckypress.com

12 11 10 09 08   5 4 3 2 1

Library of Congress Cataloging-in-Publication Data

Bial, Raymond.
The Shaker village / Raymond Bial. —[Rev. ed.].
        p.   cm.
    Rev. ed. of: Shaker home. 1994.
    Includes bibliographical references.
    ISBN 978-0-8131-2489-6 (hardcover : alk. paper)
    1. Shakers—United States—Juvenile literature. I. Bial,
Raymond. Shaker home. II. Title.
BX9784.B53 2008
289'.8—dc22
                                    2007043579

This book is printed on acid-free paper meeting
the requirements of the American National Standard
for Permanence in Paper for Printed Library Materials.

Manufactured in China.

Member of the Association of
American University Presses

The Shaker Village is lovingly dedicated to my wife, Linda, and my children, Anna, Sarah, and Luke, who accompanied me in making photographs for this book.

Whether wandering through the Shaker dwellings, walking through a nearby woods brightened with wild-flowers, or strolling around the village at dusk, being with them on these journeys has been one of the most delightful experiences of my life.

Whether in Sabbathday Lake, Maine, or Pleasant Hill, Kentucky, Shaker villages seem far removed from the rest of the world. To the Shakers who once inhabited these places—and to the handful still living in New England—each community served as a retreat from the world and the center of their universe.

Seen from a distance, a cluster of trim buildings is the first indication that the Shakers pursued a unique way of life. Not only are the buildings solidly constructed with thick stone foundations, but everything from the lines of the roofs to the placement of the windows expresses simplicity and grace. The Shakers sought perfection in their lives, intending to create heaven on earth, and the buildings indeed have a light, airy feel about them. As one brother explained, "We think that man cannot hope to attain a spiritual heaven until he first creates a heaven here on earth."

Visitors who stroll along the paths lined with trees, wade through the undulating green fields, or wander through the buildings can still feel the presence of the community of souls who once worked and worshipped in these villages. The efforts of the Shakers to create a utopian society are reflected in everything from the elegant sweep of a picket fence to the ingenious workings of a door handle.

Known formally as the United Society of Believers in Christ's Second Appearing, the Shakers are the oldest communal society in America. For more than two hundred years, they lived in these secluded villages, sharing quiet lives and striving for perfection in every detail of living, from tending gardens to making furniture.

From Maine to Kentucky, Shaker communities once dotted the eastern half of the United States. Yet while the number of Shakers has declined, other people have become increasingly fascinated with their way of life. The Shakers have come to be widely admired, not only for their hundreds of clever inventions and remarkable creations but for their progressive values and beliefs. As Sister Frances Carr of Sabbathday Lake observes, "We'll go away in time, as will every-body. But our ideas and our way of life will never go away."

The Shakers were not always viewed so favorably. During the early years of their religion in the mill town of Manchester, England, they were persecuted. Even their name was originally a derisive term: Some of the Shakers became so excited during their worship services that they would shout, tremble, and whirl about, "shaking"

off their sins. Because many of the early Believers came from the Society of Friends, or Quakers, they became known as the Shaking Quakers, later shortened to Shakers. Although the term was used in derision, the Shakers eventually adopted it themselves. They also refer to themselves as Believers or members of the United Society.

In 1758 the Shakers attracted a young woman named Ann Lees (later shortened to Lee). Married in 1762 to a blacksmith, she bore four children, three of whom died in infancy and the fourth as a small child. Always a spiritual woman, Ann Lee turned to religion after these tragedies. In giving herself fully over to her faith, she declared, "My soul broke forth to God."

Ann Lee began to take an increasingly active role in the sect, notably speaking out against "cohabitation of the sexes." Meetings grew more animated, and outside opposition to them became so intense that at one point Ann Lee was imprisoned for "profanement of the Sabbath." Upon her release, she spoke of having had a vision of Christ. Given the title Mother, she became the leader and the spiritual force of the Shakers.

To escape persecution in England, Mother Ann and seven followers immigrated to the American colonies in 1774. They settled on land that is now Watervliet, New York. For several years they scratched out a living, failing to attract new members. However, Mother Ann's charismatic personality gradually began to draw people. When she died in 1784 at the age of forty-eight, it was left primarily to James Whittaker, who had accompanied her from

England, to build an organization that would sustain the fledgling society of roughly one hundred members.

Father James began the process of gathering the Shakers in their own villages, apart from the "evils of the world." The year after Mother Ann's death, at the dedication of a meetinghouse in New Lebanon, New York, Father James introduced the "gospel orders." This formal set of rules for the Shakers included the complete separation of the sexes. Husbands, wives, and children were placed in their own communal "families," with all property held in common. "All men shall come and go out at the west doors and gates; and all women at the east doors and gates."

Just three years after the death of Mother Ann, Father James himself passed away, leaving Joseph Meacham in charge of the village at New Lebanon, which had become the spiritual headquarters of the group. Father Joseph introduced a formal rule that all members "might have equal right and privilege, according to their calling and needs." He selected Lucy Wright to lead with him.

Joseph Meacham and Lucy Wright continued the separation of the Shakers from the world by organizing a number of independent villages scattered throughout New England. During these years, so many people joined the Shakers that large communal buildings had to be constructed in the settlements. By 1794, eleven villages had been established in New York, Massachusetts, New Hampshire, Connecticut, and Maine. In 1805, when the Shakers heard of a revival sweeping the frontier, they sent out missionaries, and new communities were eventually formed in Ohio, Kentucky, and Indiana. At the height of the society's popularity, just before the Civil War, there were a total of twenty-four communities with almost six thousand members embracing the Shaker faith.

These Shaker villages were all similar, with buildings for particular uses: a place to sleep and to eat, a place to work, and a place to worship. The community itself was organized into families of fifty to one hundred brothers and sisters who shared a building with separate doors and stairways for men and women. Some of the stairs ascended in graceful swirls seemingly not of this world. Others were simpler, but in every case, men and women used separate sets of stairs. Each dwelling had its own sleeping quarters and dining room, where women and men sat apart, as well as its own kitchen, week-day meeting room, and perhaps an infirmary.

Anyone free of debt could become a Shaker. Those who had committed all their property to the society and fully accepted the Shaker way of life lived in dwellings named according to their location in relation to the Center Family: West Family, East Family, and so forth. Those who had not yet made a full commitment to the faith, including children, formed a novitiate order. They often lived in separate buildings, apart from the rest of the village.

Each family within the village was governed by two eldresses and two elders, who cared for the spiritual needs of the sisters and brothers. Deacons and deaconesses also helped to manage the work assignments of each family. The eldresses and elders of the Center Family governed the village as a whole. Occasionally, several villages were joined under one ministry or bishopric. At the head of all the Shakers was the central ministry at New Lebanon.

Each family managed its workshops and tended its own crops, garden, and livestock. Occasionally, a family had its own schoolhouse and its own store for selling goods, but generally the families shared a schoolhouse and other buildings, such as barns and shops. Most villages also had a trustees' house, where designated trustees sold goods to "the world's people," as non-Shakers were called. By allowing

trustees to manage their business affairs, the other Shakers could remain separate.

The meetinghouse where the Shakers worshipped through song and dance on Sundays stood at the very center of the village. Shakers participated in services after breakfast and again following the noon meal. They spent the rest of the Sabbath refreshing themselves through meditation and relaxation. Like other Shaker buildings, the meetinghouse had separate doors for men and women. Although it was considered the most important building in the village, it was a plain structure and lacked the spire of traditional churches.

For many years, the Shakers not only recruited adult members but also accepted orphans and children whose parents could not care for them. When they came of age, these children decided whether to stay or leave the village. Other people joined the Shakers during hard economic times or bad weather. Appropriately called bread-and-butter Shakers and winter Shakers, they usually left when conditions outside the community improved. Many Shakers came and went over the years. Those who departed during the day were given provisions and a little money, but many others slipped off in the dark of night.

The Shakers may have been the most successful communal society in America, but given the size of the general population, their numbers, even in their heyday, were still quite small. Following the

Civil War, the sect steadily declined to only about a thousand members at the turn of the century. Now there are barely a handful. Over the years, the Shakers have been criticized for some of their beliefs, such as the separation of the sexes, the breaking up of natural families, and the communal sharing of goods. Difficulties also arose when a member who wished to leave the society wanted property returned or compensation for work in the community. What was so appealing about the small Shaker sect that it is nonetheless held in such high esteem?

Today the Shakers are admired for their early belief in the equality of all people, regardless of race or sex. Their founder was a woman, and early in their history they were organized with both men and women as leaders. African Americans were welcomed into the society, and a number of former slaves became members, especially in the South. The Shakers were also committed to pacifism. They refused to take part in wars, from the American Revolution to the Civil War. During the Civil War, the Kentucky communities were frequently occupied and required to provide food and shelter for the armies of both sides.

Throughout the nineteenth century and continuing to the present day, Shakers have always been highly respected for their character, their way of life, and their humanity—all of which are clearly reflected in their surroundings and their many handiworks.

If they were to separate themselves from the world, the Shakers knew from their early days at Watervliet that they would have to farm the land to make their villages self-sufficient. As one brother wrote in his journal, "Only the simple labors and manners of a farming people can hold a community together." At first, they barely survived, but gradually, through hard work, thrift, and application of scientific methods, Shakers brought their lands, in the words of one brother, from "rugged barrenness to smiling fertility and beauty." They sold their surplus farm produce to "the world's people." By the early 1800s, they also began to market goods put up in their kitchens, such as applesauce, dried apples, dried sweet corn, jams, and preserves.

At about the same time, the Shakers entered the garden seed business. They were among the first people to package seeds, and they earned a reputation for seeds of the highest quality. Within a few years, they were peddling seeds on established routes from New England through the South. Also important was the growing of medicinal herbs. First published in 1831, their herb catalog featured 154 herbs, barks, roots, and seeds.

Just as they carefully tended their gardens and fields, the Shakers raised the finest livestock. They were among the first people to breed farm animals scientifically, and they imported high-quality cattle and sheep from England to improve their herds. Further, they cared for their livestock as lovingly as they did everything else in their lives. As one Shaker brother wrote, "A man of kindness to his beast is kind. Brutal actions show a brutal mind."

The Shakers also became widely known for their inventive spirit. "A mania has seemed to take hold of some of the brothers for inventing and being skillful mechanics, and they are successful," a Shaker newsletter reported. "It is rumored that one of our members is now studying out a plan for a flying machine." Although it was left to the Wright brothers to perfect that invention, over the years

Shakers designed or improved hundreds of practical devices. They became so accomplished that people often assumed that any new invention was of Shaker origin. Just as the Shakers were generous to those in need, they patented few of these inventions so that they might be fully shared with the world.

Many of these inventions, such as the hay rake, the mower, and a special plow for working on hills, helped ease the Shakers' labor. Among the many gadgets and tools in their workshops were the circular saw and an improved spinning wheel, as well as a special loom for making narrow tapes for chair seats. Other inventions included the washing machine and several kinds of clothespins. The Shakers were also among the first people to use metal nibs in place of quills on their pens.

Much of the ingenuity of the Shakers reflected their deep sense of community and shared labor, as illustrated by their many inventions for the kitchen. Because the women prepared three meals a day for large groups of people, they devised many gadgets to lighten the work, including the slotted spoon, a pea sheller, the cheese press, and a machine for washing potatoes. When making large batches of pies, the sisters used double rolling pins to roll out twice as much dough. They relied on an ingenious apple peeler with a screw handle and a corer. Sixty pies at a time could be baked in the large revolving ovens that they also invented.

The Shakers were committed to eating good, wholesome food; they believed that the soul could thrive only in a sound, healthy body. "It takes a whole man or woman to be a Shaker," they said, pointing to the longevity of their members. Frugal people, members were admonished to "Shaker your plates," which meant to clean them. The Shakers were among the first to use precise measurements of ingredients, and in 1796 they published one of the first cookbooks in America. They also became leaders in developing new techniques to preserve foods.

A notable tenet of the Shaker way of life was cleanliness. Mother Ann advised, "Clean your rooms well; for good spirits will not live where there is dirt. There is no dirt in heaven." The admonition was further reinforced by the Millennial Laws of 1821 (revised 1845): "No one should carelessly pass over small things, as a pin, a kernel of grain, etc. thinking it too small to pick up, for if we do, our Heavenly Father will consider us too small for him to bestow his blessing upon."

The flat broom, the most familiar of Shaker inventions, was put to such good use that it came to symbolize Shaker life. Daily cleaning actually began before breakfast, when the sisters swept their own and the brothers' rooms. Each day concluded with the brothers' sweeping up their workshops. The Shakers installed wooden pegs on strips along each wall, usually about six feet from the floor. Chairs, brooms, hats, cloaks, and many other domestic articles were hung from the pegs to provide convenient storage and to make sweeping easier.

Chairs, tables, candle stands, and other furniture were designed to express the simplicity of Shaker life, as well as to ease dusting, and beds were fitted with rollers to facilitate cleaning under them. Often furniture, including chests of drawers and cabinets, was built directly into the walls so that they would have no flat surfaces to collect dust. The Shaker quest for perfection was also expressed in a sense of order. "A place for everything, and everything in its place," became a popular saying. Desks, chests, and tables had drawers for specific articles, whether needles and thread or packages of seeds.

Commitment for the Shakers began early in the morning—at four or five in the summer and an hour later in the winter. On rising, they knelt a few moments in silent prayer; then the sisters tidied up the rooms and made beds. The sisters assigned to the kitchen started breakfast while the brothers did chores in the barns and planned the day's labor in the workshops.

At the ringing of the bell at six or seven o'clock, depending on the time of year, sisters and brothers gathered for meditation, then filed, women in one line and men in another, into the dining room. They took their separate places on either side of the room, offered a silent prayer, and quietly ate their breakfast.

Afterward, the children attended school or worked with the adults. (Girls attended school in the summer, and boys, in the winter). The sisters set off for assigned work in the kitchen, garden, dairy, laundry, or one of the workshops. Although best known for their furniture and small wares, the Shakers also engaged in many traditional crafts, such as making candles and spinning wool. The sisters might also package seeds or prepare herbal medicines.

Some of the men headed for the orchards, fields, or barns. Others entered the workshops, where they made chairs, tables, or perfectly symmetrical oval boxes. Or they might engage in traditional crafts, such as making brooms or buckets.

The Shakers switched jobs every couple of months so that they could enjoy some variety. Whatever a brother or sister was assigned

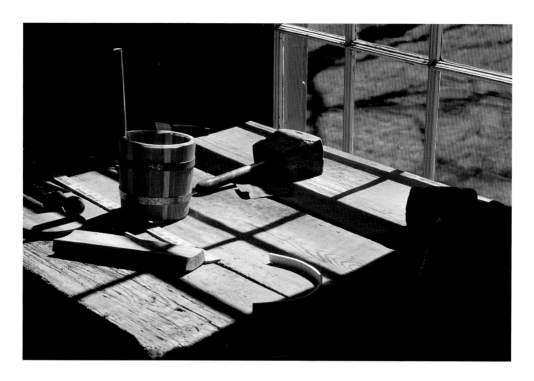

to do, the work was satisfying and often related to the kind of work to which he or she was best suited. Everyone kept busy, as one visitor reported, "in an easy kind of rhythm." Seasonal work, such as gathering nuts and berries, husking corn, and making maple syrup, also provided an enjoyable change of pace.

Not only did the Shakers surround themselves with lovely objects of their own creation, they also designed their rooms to be filled with light and fresh air from large windows. Many doors had small windowpanes that could be opened as well. "Fresh air is the Shaker medicine," a visitor observed.

The abundant light that enhanced their quality of life also allowed the Shakers to work without wasting candles and lamp fuel. What a contrast such rooms must have been to the dingy mills of

Manchester. While the Industrial Revolution was sweeping across Europe and America and people were moving into a world of darkness in factories and mines, the Shakers worked quietly in brilliant light. Perhaps part of their appeal—then and now—is their ability to lead pleasant lives rooted in agriculture and cottage industries, creating good and useful objects with their own hands.

Although the Shakers did not carry watches and rarely used clocks—devices on which factories were becoming dependent—they valued every second of their lives. Mother Ann advised, "You must not waste one moment of time, for you have none to spare." At the ringing of the bell just before noon, the brothers and sisters paused for lunch; then they resumed their labors until they sat down to a light dinner around six o'clock.

In the evening the brothers and sisters might complete a few tasks, after which they withdrew to their rooms. News from other villages relayed in letters and by visitors was shared at these times. The brothers and sisters also worshipped or practiced dances. They usually retired for the night around nine in the winter and ten in the summer.

Occasionally, Shaker sisters and brothers met together in union meetings. Sitting face to face, several feet apart, they discussed subjects of common interest or sang together, then shared refreshments.

Sunday services were devoted almost exclusively to singing and dancing. In their early years, the Shakers were known for whirling and free dancing, but by the 1820s their movements had become formal patterns, most often with brothers and sisters facing each other, hands cupped upward to accept gifts from God. Singing was very important to the Shakers, and members received several thousand gifts of songs through inspiration. Of these, "Simple Gifts" is the best known and perhaps most accurately captures the spirit of what it meant to be a Shaker:

SIMPLE GIFTS

'Tis the gift to be simple, 'tis the gift to be free,

'Tis the gift to come down where we ought to be.

And when we find ourselves in the place just right,

'Twill be in the valley of love and delight.

When true simplicity is gain'd,

To bow and to bend we shan't be ashamed,

To turn, turn will be our delight

Till by turning, turning, we come round right.

Although work and worship were blended into every detail of their lives, the Shakers also enjoyed many breaks from their daily routine, such as fishing, picnics, hiking, and carriage rides. They were also known to appreciate a little humor, even at their own expense.

In the early years, Shakers had no clothing restrictions and simply wore the clothes they had brought with them. Later, dress codes specified color, material, and style to ensure that all Shakers dressed alike, to emphasize the equality of the members of the community. Different garments were worn for work, everyday purposes, and Sunday. Although styles and colors varied over time, sisters generally wore long, plain dresses with pleated skirts, shoulder kerchiefs and capes, small white caps, and palm leaf or straw bonnets covered with silk. Like many colonial Americans, the early brothers wore breeches and long hose, which were later replaced by trousers. Jacket colors varied over the years from gray to blue, with wide-brimmed hats made of wool, fur, or straw.

While the Shakers are interesting because of their unique way of life, they are perhaps best known for their many splendid creations, notably their furniture (including ladder-back chairs, tables, candle stands, and desks) and small wares (from baskets, barrels, and buckets to nesting oval boxes). Mother Ann urged her followers to "do all your work as though you had a thousand years to live on earth, and as you would if you knew you must die tomorrow." Shakers were to "put your hands to work and your hearts to God."

Everything made by the Shakers was intended to be simple and practical. In their view, "Anything may be called perfect which

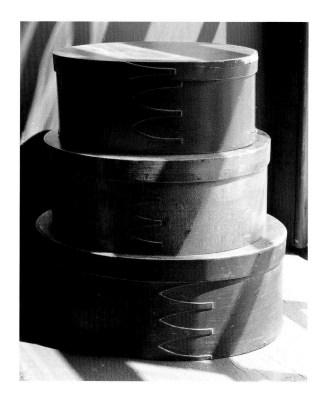

perfectly answers the purpose for which it was designed." The Shakers expressed their devotion to God by striving for perfection in their handiworks. Edward Deming Andrews described their work as "religion in wood," and Thomas Merton once said, "The peculiar grace of a Shaker chair is due to the fact that it was made by someone capable of believing that an angel might come and sit on it."

Today, Shaker furniture and small wares are considered works of art and command high prices at auctions. This dismays the few remaining Shakers, who did not create the objects to have material value. "I don't want to be remembered as a chair," lamented one elderly Shaker sister.

As members of a communal society, the Shakers shared all property. What mattered to them was not the physical reality of the collection of buildings, furniture, and other objects but the work and worship of their daily lives. The Shakers surrendered their individuality to the community. Choosing to be celibate, they gave up marriage and family, because Mother Ann taught them that they should live as brothers and sisters.

Many people think that the Shakers dwindled in number simply because they did not marry and have children. Though children without parents were increasingly placed in orphanages, a larger cause was that by the late 1800s, Shaker communities could no longer compete in the marketplace with mass-produced factory goods. Also, following the Civil War, people were drawn to the bustle of growing cities, away from the quiet farms and villages that were the essence of Shaker life.

Mother Ann predicted the decline of the Shakers: "There will come a time when there won't be enough Believers to bury their own dead. When only five are left, then there will be a revival." Perhaps the Shakers will again attract new members, but what is certain is that they have vastly enriched our world with the work of their hands and the beliefs of their hearts and minds.

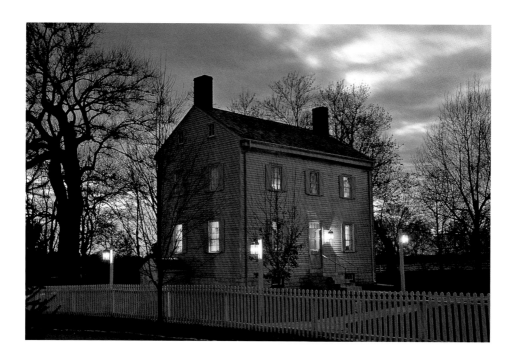

ACKNOWLEDGMENTS

The photographs for *The Shaker Village* were made at the Shaker Village of Pleasant Hill, Kentucky. I would like to express my deepest appreciation to the staff there for their generous help with this project and for their continuous efforts in keeping the spirit of the Shakers alive. Without the excellent work they do, day in and day out, none of the photographs in *The Shaker Village* would have been possible. As always, I offer my deepest thanks to my wife, Linda.

FURTHER READING

The following books were consulted in the preparation of *The Shaker Village.*

Archambeault, James. *The Gift of Pleasant Hill: Shaker Community in Kentucky.* Pleasant Hill, Ky.: Pleasant Hill Press, 1991.

Becksvoort, Christian, and John Sheldon. *The Shaker Legacy: Perspectives on an Enduring Furniture Style.* Newtown, Conn.: Taunton Press, 1998.

Brewer, Priscilla J. *Shaker Communities, Shaker Lives.* Hanover, N.H.: University Press of New England, 1986.

Buchanan, Rita. *The Shaker Herb and Garden Book.* Boston: Houghton Mifflin, 1996.

Burns, Amy Stechler. *The Shakers: Hands to Work, Hearts to God.* Rochester, N.Y.: Aperture Books, 2005.

Butler, Linda. *Inner Light: The Shaker Legacy.* New York: Knopf, 1985.

Emlen, Robert P. *Shaker Village Views.* Hanover, N.H.: University Press of New England, 1987.

Goodwillie, Christian. *Shaker Songs: A Celebration of Peace, Love, and Simplicity.* New York: Black Dog & Leventhal, 2002.

Gordon, Beverly. *Shaker Textile Arts.* Hanover, N.H.: University Press of New England, 1980.

Grant, Jerry V., and Douglas R. Allen. *Shaker Furniture Makers.* Hanover, N.H.: University Press of New England, 1989.

Humez, Jean M., ed. *Mother's First-Born Daughters: Early Shaker Writings on Women and Religion.* Bloomington: Indiana University Press, 1993.

Kassay, John. *The Book of Shaker Furniture.* Amherst: University of Massachusetts Press, 1980.

Mahoney, Kathleen, and Lilo Raymond. *Simple Wisdom: Shaker Sayings, Poems, and Songs.* New York: Viking Studio Books, 1993.

Muller, Charles R., and Timothy D. Rieman. *The Shaker Chair.* Amherst: University of Massachusetts Press, 1992.

Nicoletta, Julie. *The Architecture of the Shakers.* Woodstock, Vt.: Countryman Press, 1995.

Parrish, Thomas. *Restoring Shakertown: The Struggle to Save the Historic Shaker Village of Pleasant Hill.* Lexington: University Press of Kentucky, 2005.

Raschka, Christopher. *Simple Gifts: A Shaker Hymn.* New York: Holt, 1998.

Pearson, Elmer R., and Julia Neal. *The Shaker Image.* 2nd ed. Annotated by Magda Gabor Hotchkiss. Pittsfield, Mass.: Hancock Shaker Village, 1994.

Rieman, Timothy D., and Jean M. Burks. *The Complete Book of Shaker Furniture.* New York: Abrams, 1993.

——. *The Encyclopedia of Shaker Furniture.* Atglen, Penn.: Schiffer, 2003.

Rocheleau, Paul, and June Sprigg. *Shaker Built: The Form and Function of Shaker Architecture.* New York: Monacelli Press, 1994.

Sprigg, June. *By Shaker Hands.* New York: Knopf, 1975.

——. *Shaker Design.* New York: Whitney Museum of American Art, 1986.

Sprigg, June, and Nardi Reeder Campion. *Mother Ann Lee: Morning Star of the Shakers.* Hanover, N.H.: University Press of New England, 1990.

Starbuck, David R., and Scott Swank. *A Shaker Family Album: Photographs from the Collection of Canterbury Shaker Village.* Hanover, N.H.: University Press of New England, 1998.

Stein, Stephen J. *The Shaker Experience in America: A History of the United Society of Believers.* New Haven, Conn.: Yale University Press, 1992.

Van Kolken, Diana. *Introducing the Shakers: An Explanation and Directory.* Bowling Green, Ky.: Gabriel's Horn, 1985.

CHILDREN'S BOOKS

Bolick, Nancy O'Keefe, and Sallie G. Randolph. *Shaker Inventions.* New York: Walker, 1990.

Bolick, Nancy O'Keefe, Sallie G. Randolph, and Laura LoTurco. *Shaker Villages.* New York: Walker, 1993.

Faber, Doris. *The Perfect Life: The Shakers in America.* New York: Farrar, Straus and Giroux, 1974.

Thorne-Thomsen, Kathleen. *Shaker Children: True Stories and Crafts.* Chicago: Chicago Review Press, 1996.

Turner, Ann Warren, and Wendell Minor. *Shaker Hearts.* New York: HarperCollins, 1997.

Yolen, Jane, and Betty Fraser. *Simple Gifts: The Story of the Shakers.* New York: Viking Press, 1976.

SHAKER HISTORIC RESOURCES

For detailed information about Shaker historic sites, visit the National Park Service's Shaker Historic Trail Web site: http://www .nps.gov/history/nr/travel/shaker/index.htm.

Canterbury Shaker Village
288 Shaker Road
Canterbury, NH 03224
Phone: 603-783-9511
www.shakers.org

Enfield Shaker Museum
447 NH Route 4A
Enfield, NH 03748
Phone: 603-632-4346
www.shakermuseum.org

Hancock Shaker Village
P.O. Box 927
Pittsfield, MA 01202
Phone: 413-443-0188; 800-817-1137
www.hancockshakervillage.org

North Union Shaker Historical Society and Museum
16740 South Park Boulevard
Shaker Heights, OH 44120
Phone: 216-921-1201
www.case.edu/affil/shakhist/shaker.htm

Sabbathday Lake Shaker Village
707 Shaker Road
New Gloucester, ME 04260
Phone: 207-926-4597
www.shaker.lib.me.us

Shaker Museum and Library at Mount Lebanon Shaker Village
88 Shaker Museum Road
Old Chatham, NY 12136
Phone: 518-794-9500
www.mountlebanonshakervillage.org

Shaker Museum at South Union
P.O. Box 177
Auburn, KY 42206
Phone: 270-542-4167; 800-811-8379
www.shakermuseum.com

Shaker Village of Pleasant Hill
3501 Lexington Road
Harrodsburg, KY 40330
Phone: 859-734-5411; 800-734-5611
www.shakervillageky.org

Shirley Historical Society Museum
182 Center Road
P.O. Box 217
Shirley, MA 01464
Phone: 978-425-9328
www.shirleyhistory.org

Shaker Heritage Society
875 Watervliet Shaker Road Suite 2
Colonie, NY 12211
Phone: 518-456-7890
www.shakerheritage.org

Friends of White Water Shaker Village
P.O. Box 62714
Cincinnati, OH 45262
www.whitewatervillage.org